The Call of the Wild

Jack London

HELBLING LANGUAGES

www.helblinglanguages.com

The Call of the Wild
by Jack London
© HELBLING LANGUAGES 2009

All rights reserved. No part of this publication may be reproduced, stored in a retrieval system, or transmitted, in any form
or by any means, electronic, mechanical, photocopying, recording, or otherwise, without the prior written permission of
the Publishers.

First published 2009

ISBN 978-3-85272-153-8

The publishers would like to thank the following for their kind permission to reproduce the following photographs and other
copyright material: Library and Archives Canada/PA-005389 p102; Shutterstock p10; Wikipedia/public domain p6.

Series editor Maria Cleary
Adapted by David A. Hill
Illustrated by Stefano Fabbri
Activities by David A. Hill and Maria Cleary
Design and layout by Pixarte
Printed by Athesia

About this Book

For the Student

🎧 Listen to the story and do some activities on your Audio CD
🎧 End of the listening excerpt
💬 Talk about the story
jug• When you see the orange dot you can check the word in the glossary

For the Teacher

Go to our Readers Resource site for information on using readers and downloadable Resource Sheets, photocopiable Worksheets, Answer Keys and Tapescripts. Plus free MP3 sample tracks from the story.
www.helblingreaders.com

For lots of great ideas on using Graded Readers consult Reading Matters, the Teacher's Guide to using Helbling Readers.

Level 4 Structures

Sequencing of future tenses	*Could / was able to / managed to*
Present perfect plus *yet, already, just*	*Had to / didn't have to*
First conditional	*Shall / could* for offers
Present and past passive	*May / can / could* for permission
	Might for future possibility
How long?	*Make* and *let*
Very / really / quite	Causative *have*
	Want / ask / tell someone to do something

Structures from lower levels are also included.

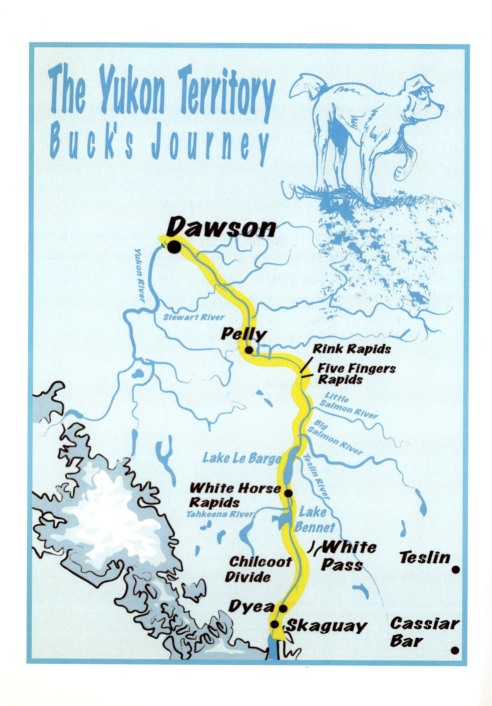

Contents

About the Author	6
About the Book	7
Before Reading	8
Into the Primitive	13
The Law of Club and Tooth	21
The Primitive Beast	28
Becoming the Leader	42
The Toil of Trace and Trail	50
For the Love of a Man	65
The Sounding of the Call	74
After Reading	93

About the Author

Jack London was born in San Francisco in 1876. Life was hard when Jack was growing up and he started working when he was 10. He did a variety of jobs, some legal*, others not, and even spent some time living as a tramp. In his free time he went to the library and spent many hours there reading. In 1894 he went back to school, and published his first short story *Typhoon* off the Coast of Japan*. Then in 1896 he went to the University of California, Berkeley, but had to leave because of money problems.

In July, 1897 he left for the Klondike Gold Rush* in Alaska. Like many others, he became very ill and came home and worked as a full-time writer. He wrote short stories and soon became successful. In 1903 he wrote the story which made his name*: *The Call of the Wild*. His next novel was *The Sea-Wolf* (1904). With his earnings* he bought a large farm in California, where he died in 1916.

London was a prolific* writer. Between 1905 and 1916 he published 18 novels and six collections of short stories, as well as a play and various works of non-fiction, including a biography. Other works were published after his death. His most famous novels were *White Fang* (1906), *The Iron Heel* (1908) and *Martin Eden* (1909). However, he was criticised for his writing technique in later life: he took pieces written by other people in news reports, etc. and changed them to his own style. Some people felt it was plagiarism*.

Glossary

- **earnings:** money from work
- **fang:** sharp animal tooth
- **Klondike Gold Rush:** period from 1896 when gold was discovered in the Klondike area of Canada and Alaska
- **legal:** allowed by the law
- **made his name:** made him famous
- **plagiarism:** copying other writers
- **prolific:** writing a lot
- **typhoon:** violent storm (in Asia)

About the Book

The Call of the Wild (1903) is considered by many people to be Jack London's finest* piece of writing, and it is widely recognised as one of the classics of American literature.

The main character of the story is Buck, a large dog, who is stolen* from his comfortable life in California and sold as a sled* dog in the frozen Klondike. Buck's new life is harsh* and cruel and he is forced to learn to adapt in order to survive. He works in a team of dogs pulling sleds loaded with mail for the gold prospectors* who have rushed to the cold north. Buck is strong and determined and soon becomes the leader. Throughout the book, as Buck passes through the hands of various owners, he grows closer and closer to his primitive origins and the "call of the wild" becomes stronger and stronger.

The story explores a number of themes which were dear to London. London took a copy of Charles Darwin's *The Origin of the Species* with him when he went to the Klondike and the story strongly reflects Darwin's theory of the 'survival of the fittest*'. This law of the survival of the fittest applies to both the animal and human worlds: both men and animals need to use their strength and intelligence to survive. London was a determinist and believed that our lives are conditioned by what we inherit* and the environment which surrounds us. So when Buck lives with Judge Miller he is a pet and lives an easy, peaceful life. His deeper inherited instincts do not appear until he moves to an environment that allows them to develop.
These themes are revisited* in London's later novel *White Fang*.

- **finest:** best
- **fittest:** in the best physical condition
- **harsh:** hard
- **inherit:** (here) qualities you get from parents etc.
- **prospectors:** people looking for gold
- **revisited:** looked at again
- **sled:** vehicle for moving things across snow
- **stolen:** taken without asking

Before Reading

Dogs

1 **What do you know about dogs? Circle the words in the box which can best be used to describe them.**

Carnivorous	Undependable	Friendly
Herbivorous	Dangerous	Useful
Intelligent	Wild	Loyal
Faithful	Domesticated	Strong

2 **With a partner make sentences using the words you circled.**

3 **There are many different kinds (breeds) of dogs, and each breed has a different use. Match the breeds on the left with the uses on the right.**

1	Alsatian	a)	a lap-dog, to be petted
2	St Bernard	b)	a dog for pulling sleds in the snow
3	Pointer	c)	a guard dog or police dog
4	Pekinese	d)	a sheepdog
5	Husky	e)	a gun dog, for hunting
6	Collie	f)	a mountain rescue dog

4 **Have you got a dog? If so, write a paragraph about it. If not, either (a) write about a dog you know well, or (b) write what you think about dogs.**

Before Reading

Alaska

1 Answer these questions:

a) What country does Alaska belong to?
b) Where is Alaska located?
c) What is the climate like?
d) What wild animals live there?
e) Who were the first inhabitants of Alaska?

2 Why did Alaska suddenly became famous at the end of the 19th century? Tick (✓) below.

☐ The film industry started there.
☐ People discovered gold there.
☐ Men started digging for oil.
☐ Ice-cream was invented there.

3 If you were going on a trip to Alaska what things would you want to take with you? Make a list under the two headings.

Clothes	Equipment

4 Would you like to live in or visit Alaska? Why/why not? Tell a partner.

Before Reading

1 Look at this picture of a husky. Write a description of it. Think about its size, shape and colour. What wild animal does it look like?

2 Think of another animal you like. Describe it to a partner. Can they guess its name?

3 The story is about a dog called Buck who first lives in California, and then is stolen and taken to Alaska. Listen to these extracts from the story. Then match them to the pictures below.

4 In pairs decide a title for each picture. Then choose one and describe it in detail. Add as much information as you can. Think of what is happening in each picture.

Before Reading

5 The titles of the chapters show us something about the changes in Buck's life and in his character. Match the chapter titles on the left with the descriptions on the right.

1 ☐ Into the Primitive

a) Buck discovers that in order to survive he must become the best dog.

2 ☐ The Law of Club and Tooth

b) Buck finally finds a man whom he respects and who respects him.

3 ☐ The Primitive Beast

c) In the new world, Buck has to deal with violence every day. The violence of men with their weapons, and dogs with their teeth.

4 ☐ Becoming the Leader

d) Buck leaves his comfortable life and is introduced into a older and more savage world.

5 ☐ The Toil of Trace and Trail

e) As Buck gets closer to the wild and primitive world of his ancestors, he increasingly feels close to nature.

6 ☐ For The Love of a Man

f) Animals are different in this new world. They have older and more natural laws and instints.

7 ☐ The Sounding of the Call

g) Buck learns to work as a sled-dog. It is hard work and he must work with the dogs in a team pulling a heavy sled across tracks in the snow.

The Call of the Wild

INTO THE PRIMITIVE

Buck did not read the newspapers. So he did not know that there was trouble ahead•. Trouble for every dog with strong muscles and warm long hair, from Seattle to southern California. Some men had found a yellow metal in the Arctic darkness, and thousands of other men were rushing there. These men wanted dogs that were heavy, with strong muscles for working hard and furry coats to protect them from the cold.

Buck lived at a big house in a sunny valley in California which was owned by Judge Miller. And Buck ruled over it all. He was born there, and had lived there for the four years of his life. There were many other dogs, but they lived together in the kennels•, or inside the house. But Buck was neither a house dog nor a kennel dog. The whole of Judge Miller's land was his. Buck was king – king over all the creeping•, crawling•, flying things of Judge Miller's lands, humans included.

His father, Elmo, a huge St Bernard, had been the judge's inseparable• companion. And when he died, Buck took his father's place. He was not so large – he weighed only sixty kilograms – for his mother, Shep, had been a Scottish sheepdog. He had had a good life and he was proud of himself, for he had not become a house dog. Hunting and other outdoor activities had hardened• his muscles, and swimming had made him healthy.

Glossary

- **crawling:** moving on all four legs, close to the ground
- **creeping:** moving close to the ground
- **hardened:** made hard
- **inseparable:** impossible to separate
- **kennels:** little houses for dogs to sleep in
- **trouble ahead:** problems in the near future

This was Buck in the autumn of 1897, when the discovery of gold in the Klondike brought men from everywhere to the frozen north. But Buck did not read the newspapers. And he did not know that Manuel, one of the gardener's helpers, was not a good man. Manuel gambled • and wasted • the little money he had. And one time when the judge was away on business, and his sons were busy with an athletics club, Manuel did something terrible. No one saw him and Buck go off on what Buck thought was a walk. No one saw them arrive at the railway station, where Manuel sold Buck to a man who was waiting for him.

Manuel put a rope • round Buck's neck, under his collar. Buck accepted this because he knew Manuel, but when the rope was given to another man, he growled • dangerously. And when the rope was tightened round his neck, he started to choke • and jumped at the man in anger. The man fought him off and forced Buck to lie on his back, and tightened the rope even more. Buck had never been treated so badly • in his life, and he had never been so angry. Then his strength drained away • and. he soon became unconscious •. He was still unconscious when the train arrived and the two men threw him into the baggage car.

TRUST
Buck goes with Manuel because he trusts him.
But Manuel betrays Buck's trust.
Who do you trust?
Has anyone ever betrayed your trust?

Glossary

- **choke:** be unable to breathe
- **drained away:** slowly went away
- **gambled:** risked money on the result of a game or sport
- **growled:** made a low angry sound
- **rope:** thick cord
- **treated so badly:** subjected to bad behaviour from someone else
- **unconscious:** not awake or capable of reacting
- **wasted:** used badly; lost

The Call of the Wild

When he woke up he heard a whistle* blow, and he knew where he was because he had often travelled by train with the judge. He opened his eyes, and he was filled with the full anger of a kidnapped* king. The man jumped for the rope, but Buck was too quick for him. He closed his teeth on the man's hand, and held on until he was choked unconscious again.

Later the man, his hand wrapped* in a bloody handkerchief, and his right trouser leg torn from knee to ankle, went into a San Francisco bar on the Waterfront*. He talked to the barman.

Buck was dazed* with horrible pains in his throat and on his tongue. He was thrown down and choked repeatedly, until they managed to cut the brass* collar off his neck. Then the rope was removed and he was pushed into a cage. He lay there for the rest of the night, feeling angry. He could not understand what it all meant. What did these strange men want with him? Why were they keeping him in this small box? He felt worried that something bad was going to happen to him soon. He jumped up several times in the night, expecting to see the judge or his sons come in, but each time it was only the barman checking on him.

- **brass:** a shiny yellow metal
- **dazed:** feeling confused and unable to think
- **kidnapped:** taken away by force
- **the Waterfront:** houses and shops near the river
- **whistle:**
- **wrapped:** covered

15

Buck passed through many hands* in that cage. He travelled by wagon and ferry boat with other boxes to the railway station, where he was put on an express train. For two days and nights he travelled north, without food and drink. And all the time Buck grew more and more angry. He was desperate for a drink to ease* his swollen* throat and tongue. But he decided that nobody would ever put a rope around his neck again. His anger would be directed against the first person who tried to hurt him. His eyes became red, and he changed into a raging devil. He was so changed that the judge would not have recognised him.

After two days he was carried off the train in Seattle into a small, high-walled yard. There a fat man in a red sweater broke open the cage with a small axe*, while holding a club* in the other hand. When there was a big enough opening, Buck jumped out like a red-eyed devil, straight at the fat man. But in mid-air, just as his teeth were going to close on the man, he received a shock that he had never felt before. It turned him over and onto the ground. He had never been struck by a club in his life, and he did not understand. With a bark* that was more a scream he jumped at the man again, and again he was clubbed* to the ground. Although he now knew what was happening to him, his anger made him continue jumping. He was smashed down a dozen times.

Glossary

- **axe:**
- **bark:** sound a dog makes
- **club:** thick stick used to beat people
- **clubbed:** hit with a club
- **ease:** make better
- **passed through many hands:** was touched and moved by many different people
- **swollen:** larger than usual because of an injury

In the end he could jump no more. Blood was flowing from his nose, mouth and ears. The man came and deliberately hit him hard on the nose. It was agony• for Buck. With a roar like a lion, he jumped at the man again, but the man hit him under the jaw•. Buck rose into the air then crashed• to the ground on his head and chest. For the last time he rushed at the man but the man struck him with a clever blow• and Buck fell down unconscious.

'He's a great dog-breaker,' said one of the men who'd carried Buck into the yard.

Buck's senses came back to him, but not his strength. He lay where he had fallen, and watched the man in the red sweater.

' "Answers to the name of Buck," ' said the fat man, reading the barman's letter. 'Well, Buck, we've had our little fight, and the best thing we can do is stop there. You've learned your place. Be a good dog and it'll go well for you. Be a bad dog, and I'll beat you again. Understand?'

As he spoke he fearlessly patted the head he had recently beaten so hard. Although Buck's hair stood up on end, he did not protest. When the man brought him water, he drank quickly, and later ate a generous meal of raw• meat, piece by piece from the man's hand.

Glossary

- **agony:** great pain
- **blow:** when you hit someone
- **crashed:** fell heavily to the ground
- **jaw:** lower part of face; chin
- **raw:** not cooked

The Call of the Wild

He was beaten* (he knew that), but he was not broken. He saw that he stood* no chance against the man with the club. He had learned the lesson, and for the rest of his life he never forgot it. It was his introduction into the world of primitive law. As the days went by, other dogs came in, some quietly and some raging* and roaring like he had. And one by one he watched them being tamed* by the man in the red sweater. Buck understood that a man with a club was a law-giver, a master to be obeyed, though not necessarily a friend.

BUCK'S FEELINGS

How does Buck feel now?
How have his feelings changed?
What do you imagine will happen to him next?

Now and again, strangers came to talk to the fat man. They gave him money and took away one of the dogs. Buck wondered where they went, for they never came back. He was frightened of the future. In the end a small man called Perrault paid three hundred dollars for him, and he was led away with Curly, a good-natured* Newfoundland dog.

The two dogs were put onto a ship where they were looked after by Perrault and another French-Canadian called François. They were a new kind of man to Buck, and while he developed no affection for them, he grew to respect them. He quickly learnt that they were fair men and too clever about the ways of dogs to be fooled* by them. There were also two other dogs on the ship – a large, snow-white dog called Spitz who was quite difficult, and stole Buck's food, and a gloomy, quiet dog called Dave who wasn't interested in anything.

- **beaten:** (here) defeated
- **fooled:** tricked
- **good-natured:** kind and friendly
- **raging:** fighting in an angry way
- **stood:** (here) had
- **tamed:** domesticated; made to obey

As the ship moved northwards the weather grew steadily• colder. Eventually the ship stopped, and François tied the dogs together and brought them onto the deck•. At the first step upon the cold surface, Buck's feet sank• into something that was white and soft like mud. He jumped back with a bark. More of this white stuff• was falling through the air. He shook himself, but more of it fell upon him. He sniffed• it curiously, then licked some up with his tongue. It was like fire, and the next instant it was gone. This puzzled• him. He tried it again, with the same result. The people watching him laughed loudly, and he felt ashamed, though he didn't know why, for it was his first snow.

Glossary

- **deck:** floor of a ship
- **puzzled:** confused
- **sank:** went into
- **sniffed:** smelled
- **steadily:** in a regular way
- **stuff:** thing; substance

The Call of the Wild

THE LAW OF CLUB AND TOOTH

Buck's first day on the beach was like a nightmare*. Every hour was filled with shock or surprise. He had been suddenly removed from civilization and thrown into the heart of a primitive world. Here there was neither peace nor rest, nor a moment's safety. It was essential to be constantly alert*, for these dogs and men were not town dogs and men. They were savages, all of them, who knew no law but the law of club and tooth.

He had never seen dogs fight like these, and his first experience taught him an unforgettable lesson. He was fortunate that it was Curly who was the victim, not himself. Curly, in her friendly way, tried to make friends with a husky* dog. The dog was the size of a full-grown wolf, but not half as large as Curly was. There was no warning*: only a fast jump, a metallic cut of teeth, and a jump back. Curly's face was ripped open* from eye to mouth.

It was wolf fighting, to strike* and jump away, but there was more to it than this. Thirty or forty huskies ran to watch. They surrounded the fighters in a silent, watching circle, all licking their lips. Curly rushed at the husky, who struck again and jumped away. He met her next rush with his chest in a strange way that knocked her over. She never got up again. This was what the watching huskies had waited for. They closed in on her, snarling* and yelping*. Curly was buried, screaming in pain, under the dogs' bodies.

- **alert:** quick-thinking
- **husky:** type of dog with long thick hair used in cold places
- **nightmare:** frightening dream
- **ripped open:** cut apart violently
- **snarling:** making an angry sound
- **strike:** hit
- **warning:** sign to be careful
- **yelping:** making small short sounds as if in pain

It was so sudden and unexpected that Buck was surprised. He saw Spitz watching, laughing. François jumped into the middle of the dogs, helped by three men with clubs and the dogs soon ran away. But Curly lay lifeless• in the bloody snow. This scene often came back to Buck. This was the way of his new world. No fair play. Once you were down, that was the end. He would be careful not to go down. Spitz laughed again, and from that moment Buck hated him.

FAIR PLAY
What does Buck mean by 'fair play'?
How would you react in such a strange and violent world?

Glossary
- **lifeless:** dead

The Call of the Wild

Buck soon received another shock. François fastened him into a harness•. He had seen them before on horses when they were working. And he was set to work, pulling François on a sled• to the forest around the valley, returning with firewood. He didn't like it, but he was too clever to rebel•; he did his best although it was all new and strange. The other dogs – Spitz, the leader, and Dave, nearest the sled – with François and his whip•, soon taught Buck how to behave when pulling the sled.

Perrault brought three more dogs to make up• the team of six to pull the sled. Two brother huskies called Billie and Joe, and an old husky who was blind in one eye called Sol-leks, which means 'angry one'. Spitz attacked the new dogs, and beat Billie, but not Joe. Sol-leks' only ambition, like Dave's, was to be left alone. Although, as Buck was to learn later, each of them had another and even more vital ambition.

- **harness:** ropes or straps tied to an animal
- **make up:** complete
- **rebel:** fight back
- **sled:** vehicle without wheels for moving on snow
- **whip:**

That night Buck faced • the problem of sleeping. He tried to sleep in the tent, but Perrault and François threw things and shouted at him until he ran away. A cold wind was blowing. He lay down on the snow but the frost soon made him stand up. He walked around the camp, but one place was as cold as another. He went back to see what his teammates were doing. To his great astonishment •, they had disappeared. He wandered around unhappily, looking for them. Suddenly, as he walked round the tent, the snow gave way • under his front feet and there was Billie curled up • under the snow like a warm ball. It was another lesson. Buck selected a spot •, and dug a hole • for himself. In a moment, the heat from his body filled the small space and he was soon asleep.

Buck didn't wake up until he heard the noises of the waking camp. At first he didn't remember where he was. It had snowed in the night and he was completely buried. He was frightened and thought perhaps he was in a trap •. But then he jumped straight up into the bright light of day. He saw the camp in front of him and he knew where he was. Everything came back to him from the walk with Manuel, to the hole he had dug for himself the night before.

When François saw Buck he shouted to Perrault: 'What did I say? Buck certainly learns quickly.'

Perrault nodded seriously. He was a courier • for the Canadian Government, carrying important letters, and he was anxious to get the best dogs. He was particularly pleased about owning Buck.

Glossary

- **astonishment:** great surprise
- **courier:** person who delivers letters
- **curled up:** in a small ball-like position
- **dug a hole:** made a space in the ground
- **faced:** confronted; had
- **gave way:** disintegrated
- **spot:** place
- **trap:** piece of equipment for catching an animal

The Call of the Wild

Three more huskies were added to the team, making nine dogs, and soon they were in harness and moving up the trail•. Buck was glad to be moving. Though the work was hard, he didn't dislike it. He was surprised at the eagerness• of the whole team, and even more surprised at Dave and Sol-leks, who were completely changed by the harness. They were no longer passive and uninterested. Now they were alert and active. Pulling the sled seemed to be what they lived for and the only thing that they enjoyed.

Dave was nearest the sled, Buck was in front of him, then came Sol-leks; the rest of the team was ahead in single file up to the leader, Spitz. They had placed Buck between Sol-leks and Dave on purpose, so that he could learn what to do. He was a good learner and they were good teachers, helping him to learn with their sharp teeth. But by the end of the day he had mastered• his work and François' whip hit him less often.

It was a hard day's run up the canyon•. They passed the timber line•, they crossed glaciers• and snowdrifts• hundreds of metres deep, and they went over the great Chilcoot Divide•, which guards the sad, lonely north. They travelled quickly past a chain of lakes, and late that night they pulled into a large camp at the head of Lake Bennet. There were thousands of gold-seekers waiting there for the ice to melt in spring. Buck made his hole in the snow and slept, exhausted.

- **canyon:** valley with steep sides
- **Chilcoot Divide:** a pass in the Rocky Mountains in Alaska
- **eagerness:** being ready and happy to work
- **glaciers:** rivers of ice
- **mastered:** become good at his work
- **snowdrifts:** deep piles of snow
- **timber line:** place north of which no trees grow
- **trail:** path or track across country

Day after day Buck worked hard in the harness. The team started off • in the dark and then stopped to camp in the dark, eating their bit of fish, and crawling to sleep in the snow. Buck was very hungry. The kilo of dried salmon, which was what the dogs got each day, was never enough for him. The other dogs weighed less and were used to this way of life, so they managed to keep in good condition.

He found, however, that the ones who finished their food quickly, would steal his. To stop this, he ate as fast as they did. He was so hungry that he even took what didn't belong to him. He saw Pike, one of the new dogs, steal a piece of bacon when Perrault's back was turned. He did the same thing the following day, getting away • with the whole piece. The men were very angry, but did not suspect him, and another new dog, Dub, was punished for it. Theft • was one of the things Buck had to learn to survive in his new hostile • Northland environment. He knew he had to change to fit into these harsh • new conditions, or face a quick and terrible death.

BUCK'S NEW LIFE

What is Buck's new life like?
How is it different from his old life?
What lessons has he learned to help him survive?

Glossary

- **getting away:** running off
- **harsh:** hard
- **hostile:** unfriendly
- **started off:** began their journey
- **theft:** act of stealing

The Call of the Wild

His development was fast. His muscles became hard as iron. He could eat anything. His sight and sense of smell became very sharp•, while his hearing developed so much that in his sleep he knew whether the smallest sound meant danger or not. He learned to bite the ice out when it collected between his toes. When he was thirsty and there was a thick layer of ice over the water hole, he would break it by dropping onto• it with his front legs. He also learnt to smell the wind and decide what would happen in the night, so that he always made his sleeping hole in the most sheltered place.

Not only did he learn by experience, but long-dead instincts rose in him again. The years of domesticated dog generations fell from him. It wasn't difficult for him to learn to fight like wolves, because that was how his ancestors had fought. And when, on still cold nights, he pointed his nose at a star and howled• long and wolf-like•, it was as if his ancestors were howling through him.

- **dropping onto:** jumping down on something
- **howled:** made a loud animal noise
- **sharp:** precise; acute
- **wolf-like:** like a wolf

THE PRIMITIVE BEAST

The primitive beast was strong inside Buck. It grew stronger under the difficult conditions of working life. But it was a secret growth. His new cunning* gave him self-control. He didn't fight and did nothing to provoke* Spitz.

However, Spitz never lost an opportunity to try and start a fight with Buck. A fight between them could only end in the death of one or the other. One night they made a miserable camp on Lake Le Barge. Heavy snow, a wind that cut like a knife and darkness forced them to try and find a camping place even though they were surrounded by high walls of rock. Perrault and François had to make their fire and put their sleeping blankets on the ice of the lake itself.

Glossary

- **cunning:** cleverness; ability to trick people
- **provoke:** cause anger in someone

The Call of the Wild

Buck made his sleeping hole under a sheltering• rock. It was so comfortable and warm that he didn't really want to leave it but he went to eat. When he returned, he found it occupied by Spitz. Till now Buck had avoided trouble with his enemy, but this was too much. He jumped on Spitz with a strength and anger that surprised them both.

The two dogs circled each other, looking for the right moment to attack. But it was then that the unexpected happened. The camp was suddenly full of starving huskies from an Indian village, who had smelt food. They had crept in while Buck and Spitz were fighting. François and Perrault jumped in among them with their clubs but the dogs showed their teeth and fought back. They had been made mad by the smell of food. A food box fell over and immediately twenty dogs were fighting for bread and bacon. The men clubbed them, the dogs howled as they were hit, but still they kept eating until nothing was left.

• **sheltering:** that gave protection from wind, rain, snow etc.

Buck had never seen such dogs. They looked like skeletons covered in thin skin, but with fiery• eyes and teeth showing. Their hunger-madness made them terrifying. Buck was attacked by three huskies, and in a moment his head and shoulders were ripped and slashed•. As Buck attacked another husky, he felt teeth bite into his throat. It was Spitz, attacking him from the side.

Perrault and François ran to help him. The wild, starving dogs moved away, and Buck shook himself free. Billie ran through the savage dogs and off across the ice, followed by Pike and Dub, with the rest of the team behind. As Buck got ready to follow them, Spitz attacked him again; he knew that if he fell, the huskies would kill him. He waited for Spitz's charge•, then ran off after the rest of the team.

The nine team-dogs found shelter in the forest. All of them were wounded• in several places. At daybreak they limped• back to the camp, to find the invaders gone and Perrault and François angry. Half of their food supply was gone. Nothing was left untouched. François stopped checking the equipment to care for the wounded dogs.

With six hundred kilometres still to Dawson, Perrault was anxious to get started. Now the wounded team had to struggle painfully over the hardest part of the trail – The Thirty Mile River. The river was flowing• and the only ice for them to walk on was in quiet places near the bank•. Six days of exhausting walking were needed to cover the distance, and at every step there was the risk of death to dog and man.

Glossary

- **bank:** side or edge of a river
- **charge:** an attack on something or somebody
- **fiery:** angry; full of fire
- **flowing:** moving (of water)
- **limped:** walked slowly because of painful legs or feet
- **slashed:** roughly torn
- **wounded:** hurt

The Call of the Wild

A dozen times Perrault, who was still in front, fell through the ice of the river. He was saved only by the pole• he held crossways• over his body. It was very cold, with temperatures of minus fifty. Every time he fell through the ice, they had to stop so he could build a fire and dry his clothes or risk dying.

Nothing stopped Perrault – that is why he was a government courier. Every day he took many risks. Once the sled broke through the ice with Dave and Buck. They were half-frozen and almost drowned by the time they were dragged• out. They were made to run round a fire, sweating and thawing•, to save their lives. Another time, Spitz went through, dragging the whole team after him as far as Buck, who pulled back with Dave and François to stop the sled going in. On another occasion, the ice cracked before and behind, and the only way to get out was up the rocky cliff face•. The dogs were pulled up one by one on a long rope. They then had to look for somewhere to get back down. That day, they only travelled a few hundred metres along the river.

PERRAULT AND FRANÇOIS

What type of men are Perrault and Francois?

With a partner think of three adjectives to describe them.

- • **cliff face:** side of high rocks
- • **crossways:** across
- • **dragged:** pulled
- • **pole:** long, thin piece of wood
- • **thawing:** melting; when ice or snow become water

By the time they reached the Teslin River and good ice, Buck and the other dogs were exhausted. Perrault, to make up lost time, pushed them hard. The first day they covered fifty kilometres to Big Salmon; the next day fifty more to Little Salmon; and the third day sixty kilometres, which brought them very close to the Five Fingers.

Buck's feet were not as hard as the huskies' feet and all day long he limped in pain. Once camp was made he lay down like a dead dog, and even though he was hungry, he wouldn't move to receive his food. So François had to bring it to him. He also rubbed• Buck's feet for half an hour each night. And used the tops of his own boots to make four shoes for Buck, which was a great relief•. Buck made the two men laugh one morning when François forgot to put the shoes on. He lay on his back waving his feet in the air, and refused to move until they had been put on. Later his feet grew hard, and the worn-out• shoes were thrown away.

Glossary

- **relief:** less pain or discomfort
- **rubbed:** touched repeatedly
- **worn-out:** old; unusable

The Call of the Wild

At the Pelly one morning as they were harnessing up, Dolly, who had always been quiet, went mad. She made a long wolf howl that put fear into the heart of the dogs, and jumped straight at Buck. He had never seen a dog go mad. He was so afraid he ran, with Dolly chasing just behind. When François whistled he came racing back, gasping* for breath. As Buck rushed past him, François brought an axe down on mad Dolly's head and killed her.

Buck crawled over to the sled and lay exhausted and helpless. This was Spitz's opportunity. He jumped on Buck and bit him twice. Then he ripped and tore Buck's flesh* to the bone. But then François' whip came down, and Buck had the satisfaction of seeing Spitz receive the worst beating given to one of the team so far.

'That Spitz is a real devil,' remarked Perrault. 'Some day he'll kill Buck.'

'Buck is two devils,' was François' answer. 'I've been watching and I know for sure. Listen: one day he'll get angry and he'll chew* Spitz up and spit* him out on the snow.'

BUCK AND SPITZ

With a partner discuss the relationship between Buck and Spitz.
Why does Spitz hate Buck so much?
What does François mean when he says: 'he'll chew Spitz up and spit him out on the snow'?

- **chew:** crush with the teeth
- **flesh:** meat
- **gasping:** making loud breathing sounds
- **spit:** throw out of his mouth

From then on it was war between the two dogs. Spitz, as leader of the team, felt threatened• by this strange Southland dog. He had known many Southland dogs, but they were all too soft, and had died from the work, the cold or of hunger. Buck was the exception. He was as strong, savage and cunning as the huskies. He could wait, with a patience that was absolutely primitive.

Buck wanted the fight for leadership to happen because it was his nature, and because he felt the pride• of the trail dog now. He openly and deliberately threatened Spitz's leadership. Once Pike did not appear for harnessing so Spitz went searching for him, and was about to attack when Buck got in the way. He attacked Spitz, knocking him over, so that Pike could attack him. Buck joined in, too. But François came and whipped Buck until he stopped.

As Dawson grew closer, Buck continued to get between Spitz and those he wanted to punish, but he did it craftily•, when François was not around. Because of this, all the other dogs started behaving badly, except Dave and Solleks. There were continual problems between the two dogs. François knew that sooner or later the life-and-death struggle• for the position of the leader would occur•.

Glossary

- **craftily:** in a devious dishonest way
- **felt threatened:** felt he was under attack
- **occur:** happen

- **pride:** sense of dignity and self-respect
- **struggle:** fight

The Call of the Wild

But there was no opportunity, and as they pulled into Dawson, the great fight was still to come. In Dawson, there were many men and countless • dogs. Buck saw them all at work. It seemed normal that dogs should work, doing all the pulling jobs which horses did in California. Every night, regularly at nine, at twelve, at three, the huskies howled a nocturnal • song, a weird • chant, which Buck joined in with. It was an old song, old as the breed • itself – one of the first songs of an ancient world in a time when songs were sad.

Seven days later, they dropped down onto the Yukon Trail, and started back to Dyea and Salt Water. Perrault was carrying letters which were even more urgent than those he had brought in. He wanted to make this the fastest trip of the year. Several things helped him. The week's rest had given the dogs time to get back to normal health. The trail which they had taken on the way to Dawson was now packed hard • because of later travellers. And the police had arranged for deposits • of food to be left in two or three places, for dog and man, so he was travelling light.

- **breed:** type of dog
- **countless:** too many to count
- **deposits:** quantities left
- **nocturnal:** night
- **packed hard:** with the snow pressed down so it was hard
- **weird:** strange

35

They did a good seventy-five kilometre run on the first day. And on the second dashed • up the Yukon, well on their way to Pelly. But this speed was hard work for François, because the revolt lead by Buck had destroyed the unity of the team. All the dogs now showed disrespect to Spitz, stealing his food and attacking him.

The relationship between the other dogs had also changed, and, apart from Dave and Sol-leks, they often fought each other. François knew that Buck was behind all the trouble, and Buck knew that he knew. But Buck was too clever to let him catch him again. He worked well in the harness, because he enjoyed the work, but it was a great delight to him to slyly • make the others fight amongst themselves.

At the mouth of the Tahkeena, one night after dinner, Dub found a rabbit, but couldn't quite catch it. In a second the whole team was chasing it. A hundred metres away, there was another camp with fifty huskies. These dogs also joined the chase. The rabbit sped • down the river, and up a valley. It ran lightly on the surface of the snow while the dogs ploughed • through it using their strength. Buck was leading the pack, but he couldn't catch the rabbit. He felt his instincts rise in him as he chased. He was at the head of the pack, running after a wild thing – living meat. He wanted to kill it with his own teeth and wash his nose in its warm blood. He was consumed by feelings deep within him, going back to the beginning of time.

Glossary

- **dashed:** went quickly; ran
- **ploughed:** ran, kicking up the snow
- **slyly:** cleverly; in a dishonest way
- **sped:** ran quickly

But Spitz was as cold and calculating* as usual. He ran away from the pack and cut across a narrow piece of land while Buck and the others followed the rabbit and the river around a U-shaped bend. Buck did not realise this. As Buck rounded* the bend he suddenly saw Spitz jump down in front of the rabbit. The rabbit could not turn, and as the dog's teeth broke its back, it shrieked* loudly. Hearing the noise, the full pack behind Buck showed their delight*.

Buck did not cry out. He did not slow down, but ran into Spitz, shoulder to shoulder. The dogs rolled over in the powdery* snow. Spitz got up immediately, and slashed Buck's shoulder, then jumped clear.

Buck knew the time had come. They circled around each other, snarling* and watching for an advantage. The huskies were now in an expectant* circle, and everything was silent. But there was nothing new or strange in this. It was what had always been, the way of things.

Glossary

- **calculating:** thinking what to do
- **delight:** pleasure and happiness
- **expectant:** waiting
- **powdery:** like powder
- **rounded:** came round a bend
- **shrieked:** screamed
- **snarling:** making an aggressive sound

The Call of the Wild

Spitz was a practised fighter. From Spitzbergen through the Arctic, and across Canada, he had fought all kinds of dogs and achieved mastery• over them. His rage was bitter, but never blind. In his passion to break and destroy, he never forgot that his enemy had the same passion to break and destroy. He never rushed• till he was prepared to receive a rush; never attacked until he had first defended an attack.

In vain Buck tried to sink his teeth into the neck of the big white dog. Wherever his teeth bit to find softer meat, Spitz's teeth blocked him. Tooth clashed with tooth, and lips were cut and bleeding, but Buck could not break through Spitz's guard. Then he tried a series of rushes at Spitz, going for the dog's throat, and each time Spitz slashed him and got away. He tried rushing, as if it were for the throat, then suddenly pulling back his head, and trying to knock him over with his shoulder. But each time Buck's shoulder was slashed as Spitz jumped away.

- **achieved mastery:** dominated
- **rushed:** (here) attacked while running

Spitz was untouched, while Buck was streaming* with blood and panting* loudly. The fight was growing desperate. And all the time the silent wolfish circle waited to finish off* whichever dog went down.

But Buck possessed a quality that made for greatness – imagination. He fought by instinct, but he could also fight with his head. He rushed as though trying the old shoulder trick, but at the last moment dived* down close to the snow. His teeth closed on Spitz's left front leg. There was a crunch of breaking bone, and the white dog faced him on three legs. Three times Buck tried to knock him over, then repeated the trick and broke Spitz's right front leg. Despite his pain and helplessness, Spitz tried to get up. But he saw the silent circle closing in upon him.

There was no hope for him. Buck moved for the final rush. The circle was so close he could feel the breaths of the huskies on his back Then Buck jumped; shoulder met shoulder and Spitz went down. The circle became a dot on the moonlit snow, and Spitz disappeared from view. Buck stood and looked on, the successful champion, the primitive beast who had made his kill and found it good*.

THE FIGHT

Describe the fight in your own words.
How does Buck win the fight?
Why is he called 'the primitive beast'?

Glossary

- **dived:** jumped downwards
- **finish off:** (here) kill
- **found it good:** enjoyed it

- **panting:** breathing heavily
- **streaming:** flowing heavily

BECOMING THE LEADER

'What did I say? I was right when I said that Buck was two devils.'

This is what François said next morning when he discovered Spitz missing and Buck covered with wounds. He pulled him to the fire and pointed them out.

'That Spitz fought like hell•,' said Perrault when he saw the rips• and cuts.

'And Buck fought like two hells,' was François' answer. 'And now we'll make good time. No more Spitz, no more trouble.'

SPITZ

Are the men sorry that Spitz is dead? Why/Why not?
Do you think they expected the fight?

The dog-driver harnessed the dogs and Buck trotted• up to the place Spitz would have occupied as leader. François didn't notice him and brought Sol-leks to the desired position. In his judgement Sol-leks was the best lead-dog left. Buck jumped on Sol-leks in anger, driving him back and standing in his place.

'Look at Buck,' François cried. 'He killed Spitz and thinks he can take his job. Go away!'

But Buck refused to move. François took Buck by the back of his neck and pulled him to the side and put Sol-leks back. The old dog did not like it and showed he was afraid of Buck, and as soon as François turned his back Buck again pushed Sol-leks out.

Glossary

- **like hell:** (here) very hard
- **rips:** cuts
- **trotted:** walked quickly (like a horse)

The Call of the Wild

François was angry. 'Now, by God, I'll fix you•!' he shouted, coming back with a heavy club in his hand.

Buck remembered the man in the red sweater and moved back, snarling with rage. The driver got on with his work, and called Buck later to put him in his old place in front of Dave. Buck moved back two or three steps. François followed him, and again Buck moved backwards. François threw down his club, thinking Buck was afraid of being beaten. But Buck was in open revolt. He wanted the leadership. It was his by right. He had earned it.

Perrault came and for an hour they tried to catch Buck. He didn't run away, but always kept just out of reach. Perrault was angry – they should have left an hour ago. François scratched his head, and the courier shrugged• his shoulders in a sign that they were beaten•. Then François went over to Sol-leks and called to Buck. Buck laughed, as dogs laugh, but kept his distance. François put Sol-leks back in his old place. François called again but still Buck laughed and didn't come.

'Throw down your club,' said Perrault. François did, and Buck trotted in, laughing triumphantly and took up the position at the head of the team. His harness was fastened, and they started out on the river trail.

• **beaten:** lost the fight
• **I'll fix you:** (here) I will stop you

• **shrugged:** moved up and down

François had always thought that Buck was good, but he had never realised how good until now. Immediately Buck took up the duties of leadership. Where judgment and quick thinking were needed, he showed himself superior even to Spitz. But it was in giving the law and making his mates live up to• it that Buck was best. He made the lazy Pike pull better, he punished Joe – a thing Spitz had never managed to do, and the team was immediately better. At Rink Rapids• two native huskies, Teek and Koona, were added, and the speed with which Buck made them fit• amazed François.

'There was never a dog like Buck!' he cried. 'He's worth a thousand dollars, by God! What do you say, Perrault?'

And Perrault nodded. He was ahead of the record time, and increasing it daily. The trail was in excellent condition, well-packed and hard, and there was no new snow. The temperature dropped to minus 50 and stayed there for the whole trip.

LEADERSHIP

What do François and Perrault think about Buck? Why is this?
What qualities do you need to be a good leader?
With a partner discuss someone you think is a good leader.

The Thirty Mile River was covered with a layer• of ice, and in one day they travelled the same distance that had taken ten days on the way there. In one run• they made the ninety kilometre section from the foot of Lake Le Barge to the White Horse Rapids. And on the last night of the second week they topped• White Pass and dropped down the sea slope• with the lights of Skaguay and the ships below.

Glossary

- **fit:** be part of the team
- **layer:** (here) covering
- **live up to:** (here) obey
- **rapids:** part of a river that moves very fast

- **run:** (here) day's journey
- **sea slope:** side of a mountain closest to the sea
- **topped:** reached the top of

The Call of the Wild

It was a record run. Each day for fourteen days they had averaged• sixty kilometres.

François and Perrault were heroes for the next three days, and the dog-team was the centre of admiration. Then official orders came. François called Buck to him, threw his arms round him and wept• over him. And like other men, François and Perrault passed out of• Buck's life forever.

A Scotsman took charge of him and his mates•, and in the company of a dozen other dog-teams they started back over the weary• trail to Dawson. It wasn't easy now, but hard work each day with a heavy load behind. This was the mail• train, carrying news from the world to the men looking for gold.

Buck did not like it, but he worked hard, taking pride in it like Dave and Sol-leks. He also made sure the team did their fair share• of the work. It was a monotonous life. At a certain time the cooks got up, fires were built, and breakfast was eaten. Then they packed up, harnessed the dogs, and were on their way an hour before dawn. At night, camp was made. Some people cut wood for fires, others brought water or ice for the cooks and the dogs were fed with fish, which was their best point in the day. After that they wandered around. There were more than one hundred dogs altogether, with some fierce fighters amongst them. But three battles with the fiercest brought Buck to mastery, so that they all got out of his way when he showed his teeth.

- **averaged:** covered an average of
- **mail:** post (letters, etc.)
- **mates:** friends
- **passed out of:** (here) left
- **their fair share:** the correct quantity
- **weary:** tiring
- **wept:** cried

Best of all, perhaps, Buck loved to lie dreaming near the fire. Sometimes he thought of Judge Miller's big house in the sunny Santa Clara valley, of the swimming tanks and the house dogs. More often, though, he remembered the man in the red sweater, the death of Curly, the great fight with Spitz, and the good things he had eaten or would like to eat.

And sometimes when he lay by the fire his mind would wander back through older lives. He would see himself with a short, hairy man who made strange sounds and was afraid of the dark. The man was almost naked, wearing a skin, and his only weapon was a stick with a stone at the end of it. And beyond the firelight, Buck could see the eyes of dangerous animals, and hear the noises they made in the night. They were the sights and sounds of another, earlier world.

BUCK'S DREAMS

What does Buck dream?
What is the 'earlier world' that Buck dreams of?
Who is the 'short, hairy man'?
Why is this world important to Buck?

It was a hard trip, pulling the mail, and the heavy work wore them down •. They had lost weight and were in poor condition when they got to Dawson, and needed ten days or a week's rest at least. But in two days' time they dropped down the Yukon bank, loaded with letters for the outside world. The dogs were tired, the drivers grumbling •, and to make things worse, it snowed every day. This meant a soft trail and heavier pulling for the dogs. But the drivers were fair to the animals through the whole journey.

Glossary

• **grumbling:** complaining

• **wore them down:** made them tired and weak

The Call of the Wild

Each night the dogs were fed first and each driver looked after the feet of the dogs in his team. Still, their strength decreased. Since the beginning of the winter they had dragged sleds two thousand four hundred kilometres. That distance affects even the toughest. Buck stood• it, keeping his mates at work and maintaining discipline, though he, too, was very tired.

Dave suffered most. The drivers couldn't understand what was wrong; it seemed to be something internal. By the time they had reached Cassiar Bar, he was so weak that he kept falling, and the driver took him out of the harness, and put Sol-leks in his position in front of the sled. He wanted Dave to rest by running free behind the sled. But for Dave this was terrible: he hated the idea of another dog in his position. He managed to keep up with the sleds until they next stopped. Then the driver found Dave standing in front of the sled in his proper• place. The drivers discussed this, because they had all known dogs who would rather die doing their work than be prevented, however sick they were. So in the end, his driver put his harness back on, and they set off with Dave in his old place. As they travelled, he often fell, or cried out with the pain inside.

The Call of the Wild

The next morning he was too weak to travel, although he crawled towards his old place. But it was the last his mates saw of him. Dave lay gasping* in the snow, desperate to be with them. They could hear him howling sadly until they went round the next bend on the trail. Then the train* halted*. The Scottish driver walked slowly back to the place they had camped. The men stopped talking. A gunshot* rang out. The man came back quickly. The whips snapped, the sled bells tinkled*, the sleds slid onwards. But Buck knew, and every dog knew, what had happened.

SURVIVAL

What had happened to Dave? Why?
Do you think what happened was fair?
Discuss the phrase 'survival of the fittest'.

Glossary

- **gasping:** fighting for breath
- **gunshot:** sound of a gun being fired
- **halted:** stopped
- **proper:** correct
- **stood:** tolerated; resisted
- **tinkled:** made a light ringing sound
- **train:** (here) number of sleds one after the other

49

THE TOIL OF TRACE AND TRAIL

Thirty days after it left Dawson, the Salt Water Mail, pulled by Buck and his mates, arrived in Skaguay. Buck's eighty kilograms had gone down to seventy. Some dogs were in worse condition. Pike and Sol-leks had hurt their legs and Dub his shoulder. All the dogs' feet hurt. They were dead tired* after their prolonged period of very hard work and with good reason. In less than five months they had travelled three thousand seven hundred kilometres.

The drivers expected a long stopover*. They themselves had covered one thousand eight hundred kilometres with two days' rest. But so many men had rushed to the Klondike, and so many wives, relations and sweethearts* had stayed home, that the mail had turned into mountains. Also there were the official orders. Fresh teams of Hudson Bay dogs were to replace the dogs which were too worn out to continue on the trail. And the latter were to be sold.

On the fourth morning, two men from the States* bought Buck and his mates, harness and all. They were called Hal and Charles. Charles was middle-aged, with weak, watery eyes. Hal was about twenty, with a big Colt pistol and a hunting knife on his belt. Both men were clearly out of place, and why people like them had come to the north was a mystery. When Buck and his mates got to their new owners' camp, he saw everything was done badly. Buck saw a woman called Mercedes. She was Charles's wife and Hal's sister. It was a family party.

Buck watched them nervously as they started to take down the tent and load the sled. The tent was rolled up* three times larger then it should have been. The tin dishes were packed away unwashed.

Glossary

- **dead tired:** very tired
- **rolled up:** wrapped around itself to make it smaller
- **stopover:** pause in a journey
- **sweethearts:** girlfriends
- **the States:** the United States

The Call of the Wild

Mercedes continually moved around, getting in the way of her men, chattering• all the time, complaining and offering advice.

BUCK'S NEW OWNERS
What are Buck's new owners's like?
If you were Buck, how would you feel about working for these people and why?
What do you think is going to happen?

• **chattering:** talking continually about unimportant things

Three men came over and watched them, laughing to each other.

'You've got a heavy load,' said one of them, 'If I were you I wouldn't take the tent.'

'Impossible!' cried Mercedes. 'How could I manage without a tent?'

'It's springtime, and you won't get any more cold weather,' the man replied.

She shook her head, and Charles and Hal put the last things on top of the mountainous• load.

'Do you think it will be all right?' one of the men asked.

'Why shouldn't it be?' Charles demanded, rather annoyed.

'It seems a bit top-heavy•, that's all,' the man answered quietly.

Charles turned his back and tied the ropes over the load as well as he could.

'And of course the dogs can pull all day with that load behind them,' said another of the men.

'Certainly,' said Hal, and he turned to the dogs. 'Mush!•' he shouted. 'Mush on!'

The dogs pulled hard for a few moments, then relaxed. They were unable to move the sled.

'The lazy creatures! I'll show them!' Hal shouted, preparing to whip the dogs.

But Mercedes stopped him, crying, 'Oh, Hal, you mustn't!' She took the whip out of his hand. 'The poor dears! Now you must promise not to be hard with them.'

'You don't know anything about dogs,' her brother said. 'So leave me alone. They're lazy and you've got to whip them to get anything out of• them. That's their way. Ask one of those men.'

Glossary

- **get anything out of:** get results from
- **mountainous:** (here) very high
- **Mush!:** what you say when you want huskies to move
- **sided:** agreed with; supported
- **top-heavy:** not balanced; heavier at the top

The Call of the Wild

Mercedes looked at them, hoping they'd agree with her.

'They're very weak and exhausted, if you want to know,' replied one of the men. 'They need a rest.'

'Rest be damned,' said Hal.

But Mercedes sided• with her brother, rather than the stranger, and said, 'Never mind that man. You're driving our dogs, and you do what you think is best.'

Again Hal's whip fell upon the dogs. They tried again, getting down low to pull, using all of their strength. The sled stayed where it was. After two efforts they stood still panting. The whip whistled amongst the dogs again, and Mercedes dropped on her knees in front of Buck, with tears in her eyes, and put her arms round his neck.

'You poor, poor dears,' she cried sympathetically, 'why don't you pull hard? Then you wouldn't be whipped.' Buck didn't like her, but he was feeling too miserable to resist her, taking it as part of the day's miserable work.

The Call of the Wild

One of the watchers finally spoke:

'It's not that I care what happens to you, but for the dogs' sakes• I just want to tell you that you can help by pushing the sled. The runners• are frozen to the ground.'

A third attempt was made, but this time, following the advice, the overloaded sled broke out of the ice and moved forward, while Hal whipped the dogs. A hundred metres ahead the path turned and sloped steeply into the main street so it would have been difficult for an experienced man to keep the top-heavy sled upright. As they turned, the sled went over, spilling• half of its load. The dogs didn't stop, and the lightened sled moved on its side behind them. They were angry because of the bad treatment they had received and the unjust load. Buck started to run and the team followed him. Hal cried 'Whoa!• Whoa!' but they didn't listen. He tripped• and was pulled off his feet. The sled ran over him, and the dogs dashed• on, adding to the happiness of Skaguay as they scattered• the rest of the equipment along its main street.

Kind-hearted citizens caught the dogs and collected the belongings. They also gave advice: halve the load if they wanted to reach Dawson. Hal and his relations listened unwillingly, made camp and looked through their equipment. Those who helped them laughed that they had wanted to take canned food, loads of blankets, the tent and so many dishes. Mercedes cried as her clothes were thrown out. In the end she threw out things that were really necessary.

Glossary

- **dashed:** ran fast
- **for the dogs' sakes:** for the good of the dogs
- **runners:** long pieces of wood/metal that the sled moves on
- **scattered:** distributed in an untidy way
- **spilling:** losing; dropping
- **tripped:** fell
- **Whoa!:** Slow down!; Stop!

When they had finished it was still a large load. Charles and Hal went out and bought six more dogs, which brought the team up to fourteen. But the new dogs were not very good, and seemed to know nothing. Buck and his comrades looked on them with disgust, and though he quickly taught them their places and what not to do, he could not teach them what to do. They did not like the harness and the trail. Most of them found this strange new environment difficult, and they were not used to the bad treatment they had received.

With these hopeless new dogs, and the old team still worn out, the outlook • wasn't bright. The two men, however, were cheerful and proud: they were doing things in style with fourteen dogs. They had seen many sleds come from and go to Dawson, but no sled had fourteen dogs. In Arctic travel there was a reason why fourteen dogs should not pull one sled: one sled could not carry the food for fourteen dogs. But Charles and Hal did not know this. They had worked the trip out with a pencil, so much food per dog, so many dogs, so many days. For them it was all very simple.

THE TRIP

What problems do you think lie ahead for Buck, the other dogs and the people on this trip?

Discuss with a partner.

Glossary

• **outlook:** prospects; future

The Call of the Wild

Late next morning Buck led the team up the street. They were starting out dead tired. Four times he had covered the distance between Salt Water and Dawson. The knowledge that, exhausted, he was facing the same trail again, made him bitter•. His heart was not in the work, nor was the heart of any dog. The new dogs were frightened, and none of the dogs had any confidence in their masters.

Buck felt that these two men and the woman did not know how to do anything. As the days passed it was clear that they could not learn. They lacked• order and discipline. It took them half the night to make their poor camp, and half the morning to pack up. They always loaded the sled so badly that they had to keep stopping to adjust it. Some days they did not even travel fifteen kilometres. And on no day did they succeed in making half the distance used by the men as the basis of their dog-food calculations. So it was inevitable that they would go short•. They tried to speed up• the journey by overfeeding• the dogs. Bringing the day nearer when underfeeding• would start. The new dogs had big appetites, and when Hal decided that the worn-out team was weak, he doubled their food. And then on top of this, Mercedes stole from the fish-sacks and fed them behind Hal's back, because she felt sorry for the dogs. However it was not food that Buck and the huskies needed, but rest. And though they were going slowly, the heavy load they pulled took away their strength.

- **bitter:** angry and full of resentment
- **go short:** not have enough
- **lacked:** didn't have any
- **overfeeding:** giving too much to eat
- **speed up:** make faster
- **underfeeding:** giving too little to eat

57

Then came the underfeeding. Hal realized one day that half of the dog-food was gone and only a quarter of the distance had been covered. And no more dog-food could be obtained. So he cut down on• the intended amount of food and tried to increase the distance they travelled every day. It was easy to give the dogs less food. But it was impossible to increase the distance they travelled when their owners were not able to get organized in the morning.

The first dog to go was Dub. His shoulder had never been treated and went from bad to worse, until finally Hal shot him with his Colt pistol. The new dogs were unable to survive on half rations• and soon six of them were dead.

And the people had problems, too. They became irritable because they were in pain: their muscles ached•, their bones ached, their hearts ached. And so they were always angry. Charles and Hal fought all the time, each one believing he did more work than the other. Sometimes Mercedes sided with her husband and sometimes with her brother.

Glossary

- **ached:** were sore; hurt
- **cut down on:** reduced
- **rations:** portions; what you are allowed to eat

The Call of the Wild

The result was an unending family quarrel•. And while they argued the fire remained unmade, the camp half prepared and the dogs unfed.

Mercedes found things especially hard. She was pretty and soft and she had been treated kindly all her life. She stopped worrying about the dogs, and because she was in pain and tired, she kept riding on the sled. She was pretty and soft, but she weighed eighty kilos. This was a serious extra weight for the weak and starving• dogs to pull. She rode for days, until the dogs fell down and the sled stood still. Charles and Hal begged• her to get off and walk, and she wept• and said they were cruel.

MERCEDES

You are Mercedes. How do you feel and why?
What advice would you give her?

- **begged:** asked (emphatic)
- **quarrel:** fight; argument
- **starving:** very hungry
- **wept:** cried

Because of their own misery, they ignored the suffering of the dogs. At the Five Fingers the dog-food ran out, and a native American traded • a few kilos of frozen horse meat for the Colt pistol on Hal's belt. It was poor food, more like eating iron than meat.

And through it all Buck staggered • along at the head of the team as in a nightmare. He pulled when he could. When he could no longer pull, he fell down and remained down until the whip or the club got him up again. His fur was in a bad state, his bones were visible. It was heartbreaking. But Buck's heart was unbreakable.

And it was the same with his six remaining mates. They were walking skeletons. In their great misery they were unaware • of the whip or the club. The pain of the beating was dull and distant. When they stopped, they dropped where they were, and when the club or the whip roused • them, they struggled to their feet and staggered on.

One day Billie could not rise. Hal had traded his pistol, so he took an axe and knocked Billie on the head and dragged the body to one side. Buck and his mates saw, and they knew that one of them could be next. Then Koona went, and only five of them remained: Joe, Pike, Sol-leks, Teek and Buck.

Glossary

- **roused:** woke
- **staggered:** walked with difficulty, almost falling
- **traded:** exchanged; when you give something for another thing
- **unaware:** didn't notice

The Call of the Wild

It was beautiful spring weather, but neither the dogs nor the humans noticed. It was dawn by three in the morning and remained light until nine at night. The whole long day was a blaze• of sunshine. Life was awakening after the long months of frost. From every hill came the sound of trickling• water, and the noise of ice falling. And in the middle of all this life, like travellers of death, the two men, the woman and the dogs staggered on their journey.

With the dogs falling, Mercedes weeping• and riding, Hal swearing• and Charles' eyes watering, they staggered into John Thornton's camp at the mouth of the White River. When they stopped the dogs dropped down as though they were dead. Thornton listened and gave monosyllabic• answers to questions, and brief advice, knowing that it was unlikely• to be followed.

- **blaze:** bright strong light
- **monosyllabic:** with one syllable
- **swearing:** using bad language
- **trickling:** moving (of water) slowly
- **unlikely:** not probable
- **weeping:** crying

'In Skaguay they said that the ice was starting to break up and that we should stop and wait,' said Hal. 'But they also told us that we couldn't get to White River and here we are.'

'They told you the truth,' said Thornton. 'I tell you honestly that I wouldn't risk my life on that ice for all the gold in Alaska.'

'No!' said Hal. 'We'll go to Dawson. Get up, Buck! Mush!'

He cracked his whip on the dogs, and one by one, they all stood up except Buck. Buck lay quietly where he had fallen. Hal whipped him again and again, but he didn't whine • or struggle. Several times Thornton started to speak, but changed his mind.

THORNTON

What do you think Thornton was going to say?
What would you say to Hal?

This was the first time Buck had failed, and it drove Hal into a rage. He got his club and beat Buck. But Buck had a feeling of doom •. He had felt the weak ice under his feet and sensed disaster close at hand, out there on the ice where his master wanted to go. So Buck refused to move. He had suffered so greatly and was so weak, that being hit with the club hardly hurt him. As the beating went on, the spark • of life inside him went down, and nearly went out. It no longer seemed to be his body where the club was falling, it seemed so far away.

Glossary

- **doom:** inevitable tragedy or ruin
- **spark:** (here) little piece
- **whine:** make a sad sound

The Call of the Wild

And then suddenly, without warning, shouting more like an animal than a human, John Thornton jumped on Hal, who was thrown backwards. Mercedes screamed. Thornton stood over Buck. He was struggling to control himself, too angry to speak.

'If you hit that dog again, I'll kill you,' he at last managed to say in a choking• voice.

'It's my dog,' Hal replied, wiping the blood from his mouth. 'Get out of my way, or I'll kill you. I'm going to Dawson.'

Thornton stood between him and Buck, and showed no intention of getting out of the way. Hal took out his hunting-knife. Mercedes screamed and cried. Thornton hit Hal's hand with an axe handle he was holding, knocking the knife to the ground. He hit his hand again as Hal tried to pick it up. Then Thornton picked up the knife himself and cut Buck's harness with it.

Hal could fight no more. Besides, his sister had run into his arms, and Buck was too near dead to be of further use in pulling the sled. A few minutes later they pulled off and down the river. Buck heard them go and raised his head to see. Pike was leading, Sol-leks was at the back, and between were Joe and Teek. They were limping and staggering. Mercedes was riding on the loaded sled, with Hal guiding it and Charles stumbling• along behind.

• **choking:** not clear; blocked

• **stumbling:** walking and falling

As Buck watched them, Thornton knelt beside him and with rough, kind hands searched for broken bones. He found nothing broken but Buck was in a state of terrible starvation. By now the sled was half a kilometre away. Dog and man watched as it crawled over the ice. Suddenly, they saw its back end drop down. They heard Mercedes scream and saw Charles try to turn and run back, and then a complete section of the ice broke and dogs and humans disappeared. A huge hole was all there was. John Thornton and Buck looked at each other.

'You poor creature,' said John Thornton, and Buck licked his hand.

BUCK

You are Buck. How do you feel now?
🔊 Tell a partner.

The Call of the Wild

FOR THE LOVE OF A MAN

Buck started to relax, lying by the river bank through the long spring days, watching the running water, listening to the songs of the birds and the hum of nature. And he slowly got his strength back. A rest is a good thing after travelling four thousand five hundred kilometres. Buck got lazy as his wounds healed*, his muscles grew again, and the flesh came back over his bones. He also made friends with Skeet, an Irish setter*, and Nig, a huge black dog, who were already living with John Thornton. And Buck came to love John Thornton.

This man had saved his life, and he was also the ideal master. He looked after the dogs as if they were his children. He never forgot to say something when he saw them, and to sit down and talk to them. Buck lay for hours at Thornton's feet, looking up into his face and following his expressions as they changed.

Buck was afraid of losing John Thornton, in the way he had lost all his other masters. But even though he loved Thornton, and behaved in ways that made him seem civilised, the primitiveness which he had learned in the Northland remained alive inside him. He was a wild thing, come in from the wild to sit by John Thornton's fire.

Glossary

- **healed:** got better
- **Irish setter:** type of dog, large with red hair

65

His face and body were covered by the marks of the fights he had had. Buck still fought as fiercely as ever, but now he fought more cleverly. He didn't fight with Skeet and Nig, who were too good-natured, and besides, they also belonged to John Thornton. But any strange dog quickly accepted Buck's supremacy• or he was struggling for his life against this exceptional• fighter. And Buck was merciless•. He never gave up an advantage or stood back from a dying enemy. He had learned well, and he knew there was no middle way. He must master or be mastered. Kill or be killed, eat or be eaten, was the law. And it was a law that Buck obeyed.

CHANGES IN BUCK
How has Buck changed from the start of the story?
What kind of dog is he now?

He sat by John Thornton's fire, a broad-chested dog with white teeth and long fur, but behind him were the shadows of all sorts of dogs, half-wolves and wild wolves. And they called to him, so that each day his relationship with people moved further away. Deep in the forest a call was sounding. When he heard it, he felt that he should leave the fire and run into the forest, not knowing where he was going or why. But then his love for John Thornton pulled him back again. But it was only for Thornton he stayed. Other people were nothing to him.

Glossary

- **exceptional:** unusually good; extraordinary
- **merciless:** cruel; without compassion
- **supremacy:** the state of being the most powerful

Pete and Hans, Thornton's business partners, understood the relationship between Buck and Thornton very well.

'I wouldn't like to be the man that attacks Thornton while Buck's around,' said Pete one day.

And before the end of the year, in Circle City, Pete's thoughts were shown to be true. 'Black' Burton, a bad-tempered and dangerous man, had been picking a fight * with an inexperienced young man. Thornton stepped between them to stop it while Buck was watching from the corner of the room. Burton punched * Thornton unexpectedly and hard, and Thornton was sent flying across the room.

Those who were watching heard a roar, and they saw Buck jumping for Burton's throat. The man saved his life by putting out his arm, but he was thrown onto the floor with Buck on top of him. Buck let go of the arm and went for * the throat again and this time tore it open. Then the crowd pulled Buck off. Buck walked up and down nearby, growling and looking for another chance to attack, while the doctor examined Burton. It was agreed that Buck had had a good reason to attack, so he wasn't punished. But his reputation * grew and his name spread * through every camp in Alaska.

Later that autumn, Thornton and his two partners were taking a narrow boat down a difficult river. Thornton was in the boat, and Pete and Hans were on the bank with a rope to stop the boat being carried away.

Buck was on the bank, anxiously watching his master. Unexpectedly, the water carried the boat faster, the rope was pulled tight, and Thornton was thrown into the river. Buck dived * into the water and soon caught up with his master. Thornton held onto Buck's tail while the dog started swimming strongly for the side.

Glossary

- **dived:** jumped into water, headfirst
- **picking a fight:** trying to start a fight
- **punched:** hit with a fist (closed hand)
- **reputation:** opinion people have of him
- **spread:** was distributed over a large area
- **went for:** (here) attacked

The Call of the Wild

But the river was going so fast, they were being carried close to the most dangerous, rocky place. Thornton managed to catch hold of a rock in the river, and Buck, with difficulty, swam to the bank, and was pulled out by Hans and Pete.

They then attached the rope to Buck's shoulders, and he tried to swim out to where Thornton was hanging on to the rock. However he got carried away by the current, and nearly drowned before Pete and Hans pulled him out. Thornton couldn't hang on much longer, so Buck tried again and went fast down to Thornton, who grabbed his neck. Then the two of them were pulled in on the rope by Hans and Pete. They had been battered• by the water and the rocks, and Buck had three ribs• broken, but he had saved his master's life.

DANGER

Have you ever been in a dangerous situation?
Who helped you?
Have you ever helped anyone out of danger?
Describe your feelings to a partner.

Later on that year in Dawson, Buck did another important thing. Thornton was in a bar one night when a man said that his dog could start a sled alone, with three hundred kilos on it. Another man, called Matthewson, said his could do so with four hundred kilos on it.

'That's nothing,' said John Thornton. 'Buck can start a sled with five hundred kilos on it.'

'What, and break it out of the ice and snow?' asked Matthewson. 'And pull it for one hundred metres?'

Glossary

- **battered:** hit repeatedly
- **ribs:** small bones that protect the chest

The Call of the Wild

'And do that, too,' answered Thornton coolly*.

'Well,' said Matthewson. 'I bet* you one thousand dollars that he can't. There it is.' And he banged a bag of gold dust down on the bar.

Thornton did not actually know whether* Buck could do what he'd said, but he had often thought he would be able to. Even so it was a terribly large amount to pull. And also, neither he nor Pete nor Hans had one thousand dollars to bet with.

'I've got a sled standing outside now, with ten fifty kilo sacks on it,' Matthewson said, 'so we can easily try.'

Thornton looked at the faces of all the men in the bar watching him. Then he saw an old friend of his who had got rich by finding gold.

'Can you lend me a thousand?' he asked, in a whisper.

'Sure,' answered his friend, putting the money on the bar. 'But I'm not sure the dog can really do it.'

Matthewson's sled was loaded with ten fifty kilo sacks of flour. It was frozen into the snow after standing in the intense cold for more than two hours. Lots of men gathered to watch, and started betting on whether Buck could move it or not. The odds* were three to one* against him doing it. Matthewson offered him another thousand dollar bet, at the three-to-one odds. Thornton and his partners only had two hundred between them, but they bet that against Matthewson's six hundred dollars.

- **bet:** put money on something (in the hope of winning more)
- **coolly:** in a calm way
- **odds:** probability
- **three to one:** (in bets) three times more probable
- **whether:** if

So Buck was harnessed on his own to the sledge. He felt the excitement, and knew that in some way he must do a great thing for John Thornton. Buck was in perfect condition. All those watching recognised this, but they still didn't think he could do it. Thornton went to Buck, and took his head between his two hands, and whispered in his ear: 'As you love me, Buck.'

Thornton stood up and stepped back. 'Now, Buck,' he said.

'Gee!' shouted Thornton, and Buck moved hard to the right, shaking the load, and a cracking noise was heard.

'Haw!' Thornton commanded. And Buck repeated the action to the left side, with similar noises from the ice. The sled was broken out of the ice.

The Call of the Wild

'Now, MUSH!' shouted Thornton, and Buck started, head low, chest near the ground, feet slipping on the snow at first, but centimetre by centimetre the huge weight slid forward until Buck had it moving steadily along. The crowd had held their breath, but now they started shouting, until a huge roar went up when he crossed the one hundred metre line.

Thornton ran up to Buck and fell on his knees beside him, and they put head against head and moved backwards and forwards together. When Thornton finally stood up tears were rolling down his face.

THE SOUNDING OF THE CALL

Buck earned one thousand six hundred dollars in five minutes for John Thornton. And he made it possible for his master to travel with his partners to look for an old lost gold mine. Many men had searched for it and many had never returned from their trip. Thornton, Pete and Hans set off with a team of Buck and six other dogs, and sledded * one hundred kilometres up the Yukon, into the Stewart River, and continued until it became a small stream high up in the mountains.

John Thornton was unafraid of the wild. He could walk deep into the wilderness *, going wherever he pleased for as long as he pleased. He was never in a hurry, hunting his food during the journey. If he failed to find anything to eat, he kept travelling, knowing that sooner or later he would find it. So on this trip, the sled was mostly loaded with ammunition * for the guns and tools.

To Buck the hunting and fishing and indefinite wandering * through strange places was an endless delight. For several weeks they would travel steadily *. For endless weeks they would camp, while the men looked for gold. Sometimes they were hungry, sometimes they had huge feasts *. Summer arrived, and the dogs and men put packs on their backs and floated * across blue mountain lakes, and went up or down unknown rivers on boats they had made from the forests around them.

Time passed as they moved backwards and forwards across this unmapped * wild country, where there were no men, but where men had been, if the story of the lost mine was true. They wandered for a summer and another winter.

Glossary

- **ammunition:** bullets for guns
- **feasts:** large meals
- **floated:** went with the movement of the water
- **sledded:** went by sled
- **steadily:** with a regular rhythm
- **unmapped:** of which no map had been drawn
- **wandering:** moving from one place to another without a fixed plan
- **wilderness:** wild place

The Call of the Wild

When spring came once more, they didn't find the lost mine, but a valley where there was gold shining through the stones at the sides of the river. They stopped wandering, and each day that they worked they earned themselves thousands of dollars in clean gold dust and nuggets•. And they worked every day. The gold was put into leather sacks, twenty-five kilos per sack, and piled outside the shelter they had built.

• **nuggets:** pieces (of gold)

There was nothing for the dogs to do, and Buck spent long hours thinking by the fire. The vision of the short-legged hairy man came to him more frequently. Now that there was little work to be done, Buck often lay by the fire, and wandered with him in that other world which he remembered.

The hairy man was afraid, always watching, ready to run when danger appeared. He walked silently with Buck through the forests. Sometimes the man would jump into the trees and swing from branch to branch, never falling, seeming as much at home in the trees as on the ground.

And along with these visions, Buck felt the call that came from deep inside the forests. It filled him with strange desires for things that he didn't know. Sometimes he would jump up and disappear for hours. He walked along dry rivers, watching the birds, reading the sounds and signs as a man may read a book. And he looked for the mysterious thing that called him all the time, waking or sleeping. It was calling for him to come.

THE CALL

What is the 'mysterious thing that called'?
Is it a real 'call', like a voice, or something else?
Think of the title of the book. Discuss with a partner.

The Call of the Wild

One night he jumped from his sleep suddenly, scenting* the air. He heard the call coming from the forest – it was a long howl, like, yet unlike, any noise made by a husky dog. He ran through the sleeping camp and into the woods. As he got closer to the cry he went more slowly, taking care in every movement, till he came to an open place among the trees. Then he saw, sitting with its nose pointed to the sky, a long, thin timber wolf*.

Buck had made no noise, but the wolf stopped its howling and tried to sense him. Buck walked out into the open, each movement showing both threat and friendliness. But the wolf ran away. Buck followed and overtook* him. He cornered* the wolf, who turned, snapping his teeth. Buck did not attack, but circled around and made friendly advances. The wolf was suspicious* and afraid, for Buck was three times bigger than him. When he saw his chance, he rushed away and the chase resumed*. Many times he was cornered, and in the end Buck was rewarded*, because the wolf, finding that Buck meant him no harm, finally sniffed noses with him. Then they played about and finally the wolf walked off in a way which showed that he was going somewhere and that he wanted Buck to follow him.

From the top of the valley they came down into level country where there were great stretches* of forest and many streams. They ran side by side, hour after hour, as the sun was rising and the day was getting warmer. Buck was extremely happy. He knew he was at last answering the call, running by the side of his wild brother towards the place where the call surely came from. Old memories came into his head. He had done this before in that other world. He was doing it again now, running free with the earth under his feet and the wide sky overhead.

Glossary

- **cornered:** blocked
- **overtook:** moved faster than
- **resumed:** started again
- **rewarded:** got a prize; was satisfied
- **scenting:** smelling
- **stretches:** large expanses or distances
- **suspicious:** not trusting
- **timber wolf:** large grey wolf

The Call of the Wild

They stopped by a stream to drink, and Buck remembered John Thornton. He sat down. The wolf started towards the place from which the call surely came, then returned to him, sniffing noses and trying to encourage him. But Buck turned round and started slowly back. For the better part of an hour the wild brother ran by his side, whining softly. Then he sat down, pointed his nose upward, and howled. It was a sad and lonely sound. As Buck kept walking, he heard it growing fainter • until it was lost in the distance.

BUCK'S DECISION

Why does Buck decide to leave the wolf?
Have you ever made a difficult decision?
What was it? Why was it difficult?
Tell a partner.

John Thornton was eating dinner when Buck ran back into the camp and jumped on him, full of affection, pushing him over and licking his face. For two days and nights, Buck never left camp or let Thornton out of his sight. He followed him at work, watched while he ate, saw him into bed at night and out of it again next morning. But after two days the call of the forest began to sound more strongly than ever. Buck felt restless •, and he thought about his wild brother, and the land beyond • the valley, and running side-by-side with the other wolves. Once again he started wandering in the woods, but his wild brother didn't come back and the sad howl was never heard again.

Glossary

- **beyond:** (here) on the other side of
- **fainter:** less strong
- **restless:** not calm or serene

He began to sleep out at night, staying away for days at a time, looking without success for his wild brother. He killed his meat as he travelled, moving with an easy step that never seemed to tire•. He fished for salmon• in a stream, and also killed a large black bear in a hard fight.

The desire for blood became stronger than ever before. He was a killer, a thing that hunted other animals, living on things that lived. He got his meat unaided•, alone, because of his own strength and ability. And he survived well in a difficult environment where only the strong survived. Apart from the brown mark on his nose and the white hair that ran down his chest, he looked almost like a gigantic wolf. He was at his peak•, physically and mentally. He saw, decided and responded, all in the same moment.

'There was never a dog like him,' said John Thornton one day, as the three partners watched Buck walking out of the camp.

They saw him walk out of the camp, but they did not see the terrible change that happened as soon as he was inside the forest. At once he became a wild thing, moving softly like a cat, almost like a shadow that appeared and disappeared among other shadows. He knew how to use the cover of bushes and trees. He could take game• birds from the nest, kill rabbits as they slept, and catch squirrels• as they ran for the trees; fish in open pools were too slow for him.

Glossary

- **at his peak:** in the best condition ever
- **game:** animal you hunt
- **salmon:** fish

- **squirrels:**
- **tire:** get tired
- **unaided:** without help

The Call of the Wild

As autumn came, the moose* appeared in larger numbers, moving from the colder tops to the valleys. Buck had already killed a partly grown* moose that he'd found on its own, but he greatly wanted to kill a larger and more difficult animal. One day, at the top of the valley he found a herd* of twenty moose amongst which was a great male. He stood two metres from the ground, and was as terrible an enemy as even Buck could desire. The moose shook his huge horns, which were over two metres across, and roared with anger when he saw Buck.

The first thing that Buck did was to separate the male from the rest of the herd. This was not easy. Every time Buck annoyed the male enough for it to run at him, several young males would run at Buck and help the big male back into the herd. But Buck was patient, like all hunting animals, and for half a day he followed the herd, attacking them from all sides, and separating the large male from the herd. As the day passed, the young males would go to help him less and less.

As night started to fall, the male was left on his own facing Buck, as the herd moved off into the darkness, and he could not follow because Buck prevented him. He weighed around 1,150 kilos, and had lived a long, strong life full of fights and struggle, and here he faced death from the teeth of an animal whose head was only as high as his knees.

From then on Buck never left the huge male moose, never gave him a moment's rest, never let him eat or drink. When the moose tried to run away, Buck just followed behind him, running easily, then lying down when the moose stood still, and attacking fiercely whenever he tried to eat or drink.

- **herd:** group
- **moose:**

- **partly grown:** not a child but not fully adult

81

The moose's great head dropped and its movements grew weaker. He started standing for long periods, with his nose to the ground, so Buck had time to get water for himself. And while he rested and waited, Buck sensed• that a change was coming over the land, that other kinds of life were coming. He heard nothing and saw nothing, yet he knew that the land was somehow different. He decided to investigate after he had finished with the moose.

Glossary
- **sensed:** felt

The Call of the Wild

At last, at the end of the fourth day, he pulled the great moose down. For a day and a night he remained by the kill, eating and sleeping. Then, rested, refreshed• and strong, he turned back towards the camp and John Thornton. He started his easy walk and went on, hour after hour, never losing his way, heading straight for home through strange country.

• **refreshed:** restored; rested so you felt fresh

As he continued he became increasingly conscious of the change in the land. There was life around which was different to that which had been there in the summer. The birds and squirrels talked about it, even the wind whispered of it. Several times he stopped and took the message in great sniffs of air, reading things which made him move with greater speed. He was filled with a sense of danger and disaster happening. And as he finally crossed the top of the hills, and went down into his valley, he moved more carefully.

BUCK'S SIXTH SENSE

What do you think Buck senses? What has happened?
What is going to happen?

Five kilometres later he found a new trail which made his hair stand on end •. It led straight towards the camp and John Thornton. Buck hurried on, quickly and quietly, every nerve tense. He was alert to all the details he sensed. They told him a complete story – everything except the end. He noticed how silent the forest was. Then his nose pulled him to one side, and he found Nig lying on his side. The dog was dead, with an arrow through his body.

The Call of the Wild

A little later he found one of the sled-dogs almost dead on the trail. Buck moved on without stopping. From the camp he could hear the faint sound of many voices, rising and falling in a chant. As he crawled on his stomach to the edge of the clearing• where the camp was, he found Hans lying dead with his body full of arrows. Then as he looked up, what he saw made him so angry that he let his passion take over from his cunning and reason. It was because of his great love for John Thornton that he lost his head.

The Yeehat Indians were dancing around the camp hut when they heard Buck's roar of anger. They turned to see an animal they had never seen before rushing at them like a hurricane•. He threw himself at their leader and ripped out his throat, and then did the same with the next man. There was no stopping him. He ran at them, biting and tearing and destroying, in constant motion. When the Yeehats tried to shoot him, they missed and their arrows hit other Indians. In panic and terror they ran for the woods, believing Buck to be an Evil Spirit.

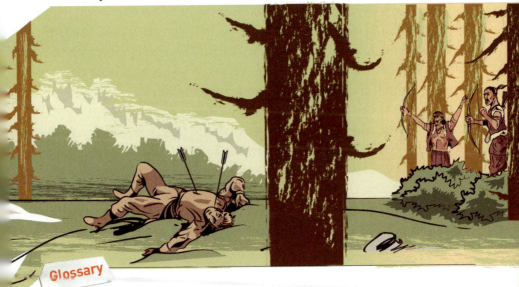

Glossary
- **clearing:** space between trees
- **hurricane:** violent wind
- **made his hair stand on end:** made him afraid

85

Buck ran after them as they raced through the trees, pulling them down like deer. It was a terrible day for the Yeehats. They ran off far and wide over the country, and it was only a week later that the last of the survivors got together again and counted their losses*. As for Buck, he got tired of the chase, and returned to the desolate* camp. He found Pete, who was dead in his blankets. Thornton's desperate struggle was written all over the earth. Buck scented every detail of it down to the edge of a deep pool. Skeet, faithful to the last, lay dead by the edge of the water. John Thornton lay in the pool's muddy* water. Buck followed his trace into the water, but he could find no trace of his master that led away from it.

All day Buck lay by the pool, or walked restlessly around the camp. He knew about death, and he knew that John Thornton was dead. It left a great painful emptiness inside him, like a hunger which no food could fill. At times, when he looked at the bodies of the dead Yeehats, he forgot the pain, and he felt proud* of himself. He had killed man, the greatest game of all. He sniffed the bodies. They had died so easily. It was harder to kill a husky dog than them. They could not match him without their arrows and clubs. From then onwards he would only be afraid of them if they had arrows and clubs in their hands.

Night came, and a full moon rose over the trees into the sky. As he lay by the pool, thinking and mourning*, Buck became alive to new life in the forest. He stood up, listening and scenting. From far away drifted a faint, sharp yelp*, followed by others. As the moments passed the yelps grew closer and louder. Buck knew them as things heard in that other world that had stayed in his memory.

Glossary

- **counted their losses:** counted how many were dead
- **desolate:** lonely and unhappy
- **mourning:** when you are sad when someone dies
- **muddy:** dirty with earth
- **proud:** happy about something he did
- **yelp:** short, high cry

The Call of the Wild

He walked into the centre of the open space and listened. It was the call, the many-noted call, pulling him more than ever. And, as never before, he was ready to obey it. John Thornton was dead. The last tie• was broken. Man and his wishes no longer held Buck.

• **tie:** link; connection

87

The Call of the Wild

THE CALL OF THE WILD
What has changed in Buck now? Why?
What do you think he is going to do?

Hunting for meat and following the migrating • moose, the wolf pack •
had crossed over from the land of streams and forests into Buck's valley.
They poured into the clearing like a silver stream in the moonlight. Buck
stood, motionless • as a statue in the middle, waiting for them. They
were quietened, so still • and large he stood, and a moment's pause fell.
Then one wolf jumped at him, and like a flash •, Buck struck, breaking
his neck. Then Buck stood still again, as the wolf died in front of him.
Three others tried, one after the other, and immediately crawled back,
covered in blood from cut throats or shoulders.

This was enough to make the whole pack attack him. But Buck was
fast and agile •. Snapping and tearing, he was everywhere at once. To
stop them getting behind him, he moved backwards, down past the
pool, and along a bank that men had made when they were mining.
Finally he got into a corner, protected on three sides and with nothing
to do but face the front.

And so well did he face it, that at the end of half an hour, the wolves
drew back •, defeated. They lay or stood, watching Buck. One wolf, thin
and grey, walked carefully towards him in a friendly way, and Buck
recognised the wild brother with whom he had run night and day. He
was whining softly, and as Buck whined, they touched noses.

Glossary

- **agile:** moving quickly and easily
- **drew back:** moved backwards
- **like a flash:** very quickly
- **migrating:** moving (usually for food or better weather)
- **motionless:** without moving
- **pack:** group
- **still:** without moving

Then an old scarred wolf came forward and sniffed noses with Buck. The old wolf then sat down, pointed his nose at the moon and started the long wolf howl. The others all sat down and howled. And now the call came to Buck and it was unmistakable. He, too, sat down and howled. This over, he came out of his corner, and the pack crowded round him in a half-friendly, half-savage way. The leaders yelped, and the pack moved away into the woods. And Buck ran with them, side by side with his wild brother, yelping as he ran.

And here the story of Buck could end. But it was not long before the Yeehat Indians noticed a change in the timber wolves. Some of them had patches of brown on their heads and noses, and a white line down their chests. But more than that, the Yeehats tell of a Ghost Dog that runs at the head of the pack. They are afraid of this Ghost Dog, because it is more cunning than they are. It steals from their camps in hard winters, takes food from their traps, kills their dogs and stands up to* their bravest hunters.

But the story gets worse. There are hunters who never return to the camp. They are found with their throats cut open and footprints* around them in the snow which are larger than any wolf prints. And each autumn, when the Yeehats follow the moose, there is a certain valley which they never enter. And they become sad when they talk over the fire of how the Evil Spirit selected that valley to live in.

Glossary

- **footprints:** signs or marks a foot leaves in the earth
- **stands up to:** is not afraid of

The Call of the Wild

THE GHOST DOG

Who is the 'Ghost Dog'?
What legends or stories are in your culture?
What legends do you know?
🗣 Share with a partner.

In the summers, however, there is one visitor to that valley that the Yeehats do not know about. It is a large, beautifully furry wolf, who is like, and yet unlike, all other wolves. He crosses alone from the land of streams and trees, and comes down to an open space among the trees. Here a yellow stream flows from old leather bags and sinks into the ground. And here the wolf thinks for a time, howling one long, sad howl before he leaves.

But he is not always alone. When the long winter nights come the wolves follow their meat into the lower valleys. Then he may be seen running at the head of the pack through the pale moonlight. He is gigantic and his great throat howls out the song of the younger world, which is the song of the pack.

After Reading

Personal Response

1 What did you think of the story? Write a paragraph describing your reaction to it.

2 Which of the humans in the story did you like best and least? Why?

3 What do you think of Buck? Do you like the dog? Do you admire him? Or do you dislike him and what he does?

4 What is 'the call of the wild' which Buck follows? Do you think it is something that all dogs can feel? Is it a positive or negative thing?

5 Which part of the story did you enjoy most? Explain why.

After Reading

Comprehension

1 **Explain who these people are and how they are connected to Buck. Write one sentence about each of them.**

    a) Judge Miller   *He was the man who owned Buck in California.*

    b) Manuel

    c) The dog-breaker

    d) François

    e) Hal

    f) John Thornton

2 **What things did Buck learn in his first few days in Alaska?**

3 **What is the significance of Spitz in the story?**

4 **What was the problem with Buck's feet, and how did François solve it?**

5 **What did the huskies do at nine, twelve and three o'clock each night in Dawson? Why is this important in Buck's development?**

6 **What helped Buck's team break the record on the way back from Dawson with François and Perrault?**

After Reading

7 What trick did Buck use to beat Spitz in the final fight?

8 When Buck lay by the fire who and what did he dream about? How is this connected to the title of the book?

9 Who bought Buck and his team when they got back to Skaguay? What were these men like?

10 How does Buck come to live with John Thornton?

11 Think of three times Buck helps John Thornton.

a) _____

b) _____

c) _____

12 Who does Buck meet in the forests? What do they do together? Why doesn't Buck go with him?

13 What happens at the camp while Buck is away?

14 What does Buck do in the end?

After Reading

Characters

1 Describe the characters of the main humans in the story:

a) Manuel

b) François

c) Hal

d) John Thornton

2 Describe the characters of the main dogs in the story:

a) Spitz

b) Curly

c) Dave and Sol-leks

d) Skeet and Nig

After Reading

3 With a partner trace the changes Buck makes throughout the story.
What is he like at the beginning? What is he like at the end?
Tell the class.

4 How does Buck react when he sees what has happened at John Thornton's camp?

5 How does Buck win the respect of the wolf pack?

6 Do you think the story has a happy ending for Buck? Why/why not?

7 Would you choose Buck to be your dog? Why/why not?

After Reading

Plot and Theme

1 **Who tells the story? Buck? John Thornton?
Another character? Who else?
Explain the reason for your choice.**

2 **How is the story told? Tick (✓)**

    a) ☐ With flashback, moving backwards and forwards from present to past.
    b) ☐ With a linear plot that moves directly from A to B to C.
    c) ☐ With a cyclical plot moving around a central event, always returning to it.

3 **What is the effect of this way of story-telling?
Think of the books and stories you have read.
How are they told?**

4 **Which of the following themes is present in *The Call of the Wild*?
Tick (✓). Find examples to illustrate each one.**

    a) ☐ The cruelty of man
    b) ☐ Loyalty
    c) ☐ Man's greed
    d) ☐ Respect for nature
    e) ☐ The importance of our roots

5 **How many years does the book cover?**

After Reading

6 **What are the main events in the story? Write the events from the theft of Buck to when he joins the wolf pack.**

The theft of Buck

_____

_____

_____

_____

_____

_____

_____

Buck joining the wolf pack

7 **Which of the following sentences describe the story best? Tick (✓)**

a) ☐ How a dog becomes wild.
b) ☐ How a dog returns to its old, natural state.
c) ☐ How humans mistreat dogs.
d) ☐ How humans are unimportant for dogs.

8 **What events in the story bring Buck closer to 'the wild'?**

9 **What does London mean at the end of the story when he says that Buck 'howls out the song of the younger world'?**

10 **Do you think that the story has a positive or negative ending? Explain your answer to a partner.**

99

After Reading

Test

**1 Read the text then look at the sentences about holidays in the Yukon.
Decide if each sentence is correct (✓) or incorrect (✗).**

HOLIDAYS IN THE YUKON

Would you like to see the home of the Klondike Gold Rush? Then visit the National Historical Park, and see what the gold miners' life was like! The seaside town of Skagway is a good place to stay, and it was the starting point for many of the miners. The weather is mild for most of the year, with no snow on the ground between March and October. The temperatures get up to nearly 21°C from June to August; June and July also have very low rainfall.

There is much to do, especially if you enjoy walking in wild country with few people and lots of wildlife. You can watch seals and whales in the sea, and bears, moose and other animals in the forests. There are also many kinds of birds and flowers to see.

The National Historical Park offers a number of different guided tours with its rangers, and if you feel adventurous, you can hike up the famous Chilkoot Trail, which was used by the Gold Rush miners. It is difficult, even in summer, and you need to be an experienced and fit walker to do it; you also need to take the right camping equipment, clothing and food. You can check what is advised on the National Park Service website. One interesting thing is that if you hike up the trail from Skagway, like the miners, you will cross the border from the USA into Canada!

a) ☐ Skagway is a good place to stay because of the weather.

b) ☐ It snows in Skagway from November to February.

c) ☐ The area is busy, lively and full of people.

d) ☐ The National Historical Park is a good place to watch wild animals.

e) ☐ The Chilkoot Trail is very easy for hiking in summer.

f) ☐ You need special equipment if you walk the Chilkoot Trail.

g) ☐ You go from Canada into the USA if you hike up the trail.

After Reading

2 Read the text below and chose the correct word for each space. Write 1, 2, 3 or 4 in the space.

The Alaskan Husky

The Alaskan husky is not really a breed of dog like a German shepherd or a poodle, but a type of dog. They are bred as working dogs to **(a)** _____ sleds. They typically weigh around 20 kg, and can have a coat of any **(b)** _____ from black to white; it is usually short. Their **(c)** _____ are usually brown or blue. The most important thing about an Alaskan husky is its speed, strength and endurance. Although husky dogs were first **(d)** _____ in Alaska in 1577 by the English explorer Martin Frobisher, they were really developed in the late nineteenth century by the miners in the Alaskan Gold Rushes.

Alaskan huskies do not make good **(e)**_____ in town houses and flats. Because they are working dogs and travel long distances, they need a lot of **(f)**_____ and very good training. They are intelligent animals, and very easily get **(g)** _____, especially if they are left alone. They are good diggers, and can easily **(h)** _____ from a garden. They are also natural hunters, and will **(i)** _____ any small animals like cats, rats and even smaller dogs.

a)	**1** push	**2** pull	**3** run	**4** ride
b)	**1** shape	**2** size	**3** colour	**4** height
c)	**1** eyes	**2** ears	**3** noses	**4** teeth
d)	**1** heard	**2** born	**3** grown	**4** seen
e)	**1** animals	**2** dogs	**3** pets	**4** mammals
f)	**1** exercise	**2** exercises	**3** practice	**4** jobs
g)	**1** interested	**2** bored	**3** excited	**4** animated
h)	**1** hide	**2** get lost	**3** escape	**4** jump
i)	**1** find	**2** like	**3** play with	**4** chase

After Reading

Project

The Klondike Gold Rush

1 Find out the true facts about the Klondike Gold Rush which inspired *The Call of the Wild*. Answer the following questions, and then use your answers to write a report about it.

  a) How much gold has been mined in the Yukon area since the first gold was found?
  b) What happened in August 1896, and why was Keish (Skookum Jim Mason) important?
  c) What problems were there in the USA that made so many people want to go and look for gold?
  d) Where did people travel from to find gold in the Yukon? What sort of people were they?
  e) What were the chances of finding gold?
  f) Why did people have to take one ton of supplies?
  g) Who checked the people arriving to look for gold?
  h) Of the 100, 000 people who went to the Yukon, how many actually got to the gold fields?
  i) How did many people become rich at the time of the gold rush?
  j) What were some of the most difficult things about the journeys they made through the Yukon?

Use the Internet to find the answers.

WEB Check the www.helblingreaders.com for useful links.